NATIONAL GEOGRAPHIC Kids

REVEALING THE MYSTERIOUS LIVING

ALIEN DEEP

WORLD AT THE BOTTOM OF THE OCEAN

By BRADLEY HAGUE

NATIONAL GEOGRAPHIC

WASHINGTON, D.C.

To Elizabeth Sofia and the Rohan cousins—B. H.

Acknowledgments

This book is the result of many people who deserve special thanks: Tim Shank at Woods Hole Oceanographic Institution, the crew of the *Okeanos Explorer* and NOAA's Office of Oceanic Exploration and Research, the GALREX Science Team (Edward Backer, Robert Embley, Stephen Hammond, Santiago Herrera, Taylor Heyl, James Holden, T. Jennifer Lin, Catriona Munro, Lucy Stewart, Scott White), Suzanne Fonda for her tireless editing work, Maryanne Culpepper and the National Geographic Television staff behind the Alien Deep series, my family and friends for their support, and Emily Kennedy for more than words can say. Thank you.—B. H.

Published by the National Geographic Society

John M. Fahey, Jr., *Chairman of the Board and Chief Executive Officer*

Tim T. Kelly, *President*

Declan Moore, *Executive Vice President; President, Publishing and Digital Media*

Melina Gerosa Bellows, *Executive Vice President, Chief Creative Officer, Books, Kids, and Family*

Prepared by the Book Division

Hector Sierra, *Senior Vice President and General Manager*

Nancy Laties Feresten, *Senior Vice President, Editor in Chief, Children's Books*

Jonathan Halling, *Design Director, Books and Children's Publishing*

Jay Sumner, *Director of Photography, Children's Publishing*

Jennifer Emmett, *Editorial Director, Children's Books*

Eva Absher-Schantz, *Managing Art Director, Children's Books*

Carl Mehler, *Director of Maps*

R. Gary Colbert, *Production Director*

Jennifer A. Thornton, *Director of Managing Editorial*

Staff for This Book

Priyanka Lamichhane, *Project Editor*

Suzanne Patrick Fonda, *Editor*

David M. Seager, *Art Director/Designer*

Lori Epstein, *Senior Illustrations Editor*

Kate Olesin, *Assistant Editor*

Kathryn Robbins, *Design Production Assistant*

XNR Productions, *Map Research and Production*

Joan Gossett, *Production Editor*

Grace Hill, *Associate Managing Editor*

Lewis R. Bassford, *Production Manager*

Susan Borke, *Legal and Business Affairs*

Manufacturing and Quality Management

Phillip L. Schlosser, *Senior Vice President*

Chris Brown, *Vice President, Book Manufacturing*

George Bounelis, *Vice President, Production Services*

Robert L. Barr, Nicole Elliott, and Rachel Faulise, *Managers*

Illustration Credits

Cover composite illustration, smoker image courtesy of NOAA Okeanos Explorer Program, Galápagos Rift Expedition 2011; ROV image courtesy of NOAA Okeanos Explorer Program, INDEX-SATAL 2010. 2–3, image courtesy of Aquapix and Expedition to the Deep Slope 2007, NOAA-OE; 5, Igor Kovalchuk/Shutterstock; 6–7, National Geographic Television; 8, Stephen Low Distribution Inc./National Geographic Stock; 10 (CTR), Emory Kristof/National Geographic Stock; 10 (LO), Woods Hole Oceanographic Institution Archives/WHOI; 10, Igor Kovalchuk/Shutterstock; 11, OAR/National Undersea Research Program (NURP), NOAA; 14, Michael Hampshire/National Geographic Stock; 14 (background), Igor Kovalchuk/Shutterstock; 15, image courtesy of Submarine Ring of Fire 2006 Exploration, NOAA Vents Program; 16, image courtesy of INDEX 2010: "Indonesia-USA Deep-Sea Exploration of the Sangihe Talaud Region"; 18, image courtesy of NOAA Okeanos Explorer Program, INDEX-SATAL 2010; 19, image courtesy of NOAA Okeanos Explorer Program, INDEX-SATAL 2010; 20, image courtesy of New Zealand American Submarine Ring of Fire 2007 Exploration, NOAA Vents Program, the Institute of Geological & Nuclear Sciences and NOAA-OE; 22 (background), Igor Kovalchuk/Shutterstock; 22 (UP), Emory Kristof and Alvin Chandler/National Geographic Stock; 22 (UP CTR), NOAA; 22 (LOCTR), NOAA; 22 (LO), image courtesy of INDEX 2010: "Indonesia-USA Deep-Sea Exploration of the Sangihe Talaud Region"; 23, D. Fornari, Woods Hole Oceanographic Institution, and R. Haymon, UC-Santa Barbara/ WHOI; 24, Stephen Low Distribution Inc./National Geographic Stock; 26, Emory Kristof/National Geographic Stock; 27, image courtesy of NOAA Okeanos Explorer Program, Galápagos Rift Expedition 2011; 28, Tim Shank, Woods Hole Oceanographic Institution; 28–29, Shank Lab/Woods Hole Oceanographic Institution; 30 (UP), image courtesy of NOAA Okeanos Explorer Program, INDEX-SATAL 2010; 30 (LO), image courtesy of NOAA Okeanos Explorer Program, Galápagos Rift Expedition 2011; 32, image courtesy of NOAA Okeanos Explorer Program, Galápagos Rift Expedition 2011; 34 (LE), image courtesy of NOAA Okeanos Explorer Program, Galápagos Rift Expedition 2011; 34–35 (RT), image courtesy of NOAA Okeanos Explorer Program, Galápagos Rift Expedition 2011; 34 (LO), image courtesy of NOAA Okeanos Explorer Program, Galápagos Rift Expedition 2011; 36 (UP), Bruce Strickrott, Woods Hole Oceanographic Institution; 36 (LO), image courtesy of NOAA Okeanos Explorer Program, Galápagos Rift Expedition 2011; 37 (LE), image courtesy of NOAA Okeanos Explorer Program, Galápagos Rift Expedition 2011; 37 (RT), image courtesy of NOAA Okeanos Explorer Program, Galápagos Rift Expedition 2011; 38–39 (UP), Bruce Strickrott, Woods Hole Oceanographic Institution; 38 (LO), image courtesy of NOAA Okeanos Explorer Program, INDEX-SATAL 2010; 39 (CTR), Ifremer/A. Fifis; 39 (LO), image courtesy of Kevin Raskoff, California State University, Monterey Bay, The Hidden Ocean Arctic 2005 Exploration, NOAA-OER; 40, Frans Lanting/Corbis; 42, © 2004 Buena Vista Pictures Distribution and Walden Media. Walden Media is a registered trademark of Walden Media, LLC. All Rights Reserved; 44 (UP), image courtesy of NOAA Okeanos Explorer Program, Galápagos Rift Expedition 2011; 44 (UP CTR), Creative Logik Universe; 44, Clearviewstock/Shutterstock; 44 (CTR), Julie Huber, NOAA Ocean Explorer: Okeanos Explorer: Mid-Cayman Rise Expedition 2011; 44 (LOCTR), D. J. Patterson, image used under license to MBL (micro*scope); 44 (LO), D. J. Patterson, image used under license to MBL (micro*scope); 45, E. Paul Oberlander, Woods Hole Oceanographic Institution.

Cover: *Lights from* Little Hercules *reveal a belching black smoker hydrothermal vent rising from the seafloor.*

Title page: *An anemone, one of hundreds of new species found at deep-sea hydrothermal vents, waves its tentacles in the darkness.*

This material is based upon work supported by the National Science Foundation under Grant No. DRL-1114251. Any opinions, findings, and conclusions or recommendations expressed in this material are those of the author(s) and do not necessarily reflect the views of the National Science Foundation.

As seen on the National Geographic Channel

Library of Congress Cataloging-in-Publication Data

Hague, Bradley.
Alien deep: revealing the mysterious living world at the bottom of the ocean / by Bradley Hague.
  p. cm.
Includes bibliographical references and index.
ISBN 978-1-4263-1067-6 (hardcover : alk. paper) — ISBN 978-1-4263-1068-3 (library binding : alk. paper)
1. Hydrothermal vents. 2. Hydrothermal vent ecology. 3. Hydrothermal vent animals. I. Title.
GB1198.H34 2012
551.2'3—dc23

2012012939

The National Geographic Society is one of the world's largest nonprofit scientific and educational organizations. Founded in 1888 to "increase and diffuse geographic knowledge," the Society works to inspire people to care about the planet. It reaches more than 325 million people worldwide each month through its official journal, *National Geographic,* and other magazines; National Geographic Channel; television documentaries; music; radio; films; books; DVDs; maps; exhibitions; school publishing programs; interactive media; and merchandise. National Geographic has funded more than 9,000 scientific research, conservation and exploration projects and supports an education program combating geographic illiteracy. For more information, visit nationalgeographic.com.

For more information, please call 1-800-NGS LINE (647-5463)
or write to the following address:
National Geographic Society
1145 17th Street N.W.
Washington, D.C. 20036-4688 U.S.A.

Visit us online at
www.nationalgeographic.com/books

For librarians and teachers:
www.ngchildrensbooks.org

More for kids from National Geographic: kids.nationalgeographic.com

For information about special discounts for bulk purchases, please contact National Geographic Books Special Sales: ngspecsales@ngs.org

For rights or permissions inquiries, please contact National Geographic Books Subsidiary Rights: ngbookrights@ngs.org

Printed in Hong Kong
13/THK/2

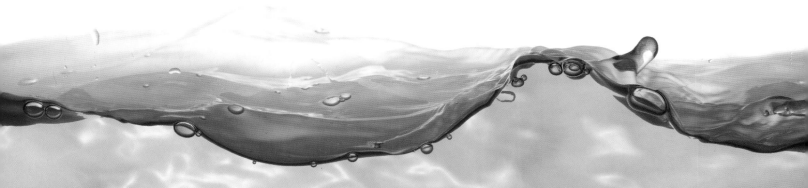

TABLE OF CONTENTS

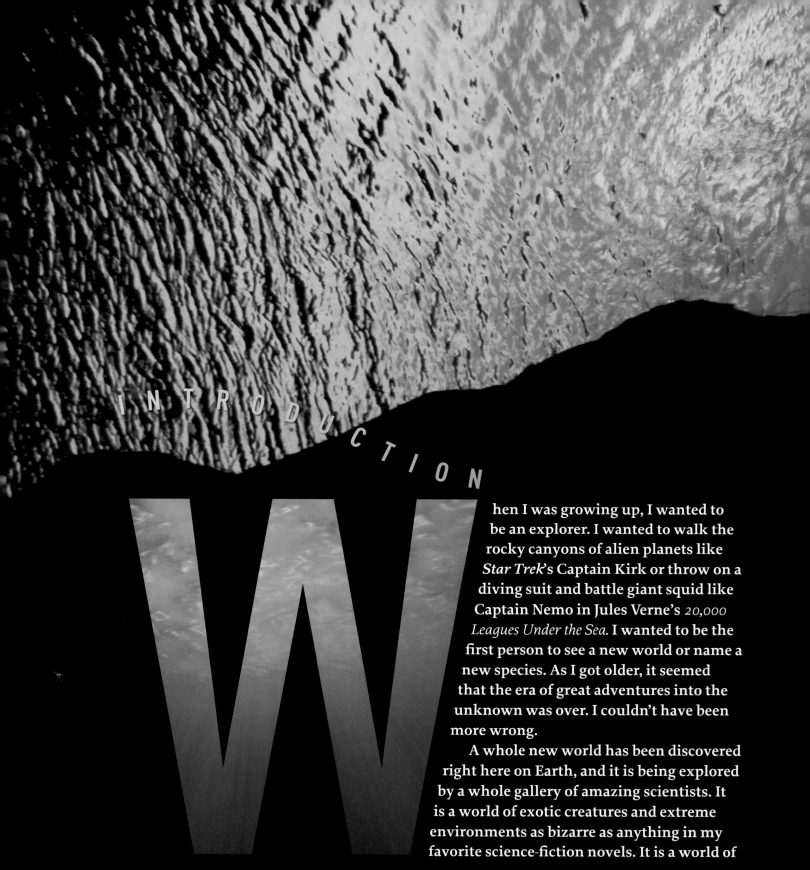

When I was growing up, I wanted to be an explorer. I wanted to walk the rocky canyons of alien planets like *Star Trek*'s Captain Kirk or throw on a diving suit and battle giant squid like Captain Nemo in Jules Verne's *20,000 Leagues Under the Sea*. I wanted to be the first person to see a new world or name a new species. As I got older, it seemed that the era of great adventures into the unknown was over. I couldn't have been more wrong.

A whole new world has been discovered right here on Earth, and it is being explored by a whole gallery of amazing scientists. It is a world of exotic creatures and extreme environments as bizarre as anything in my favorite science-fiction novels. It is a world of

A strange world far beneath the surface is waiting to be discovered.

lethal landscapes where some of the most basic assumptions about life are being questioned. Even better, it is a world that, until its discovery, scientists never thought possible: the world of deep-sea hydrothermal vents.

In the 35 years since the first one was discovered in 1977, hydrothermal vents have revolutionized our understanding of life: where it came from, how it evolved, and what its limits are. But our knowledge is still fragmentary. There may be thousands or even tens of thousands of deep-sea vents erupting around the world, but so far all of our answers come from only a few hundred of them. It's like saying you understand the world's forests because you've seen a few trees.

In this book we'll join biologist Tim Shank and the crew of the *Okeanos Explorer*, America's first research ship dedicated solely to exploration, on their expedition along the Galápagos Rift in the Pacific. They are just one of several scientific teams worldwide who are scouring the planet for new vents, new species, or other never-before-imagined discoveries that could deepen our understanding about life not just on Earth but throughout the universe.

The exploration of this alien world is a story of incredible daring, amazing discovery, and exceptional luck. New revelations occur on every dive, and understanding them will take generations.

The deep ocean is a strange world, a new world, and a world worthy of great exploration and explorers—like you.

The red color of a tubeworm comes from hemoglobin, just as in human blood.

Tubeworm shells are made of chitin, just as lobster and crab shells are.

HYDROTHERMAL VENT

A PLACE WHERE SUPER-HEATED WATER FROM DEEP INSIDE EARTH ERUPTS FROM THE OCEAN FLOOR

8

AN UNEXPECTED DISCOVERY

Thickets of tubeworms like this one astonished the scientists who found them while searching for hot water flowing from Earth's crust. Life like this wasn't thought to be possible.

T IS FEBRUARY 15, 1977. AFTER DAYS OF towing a small heat-sensitive vehicle known as *Angus* just above the seafloor of the Galápagos Rift, scientists aboard the research vessel *Knorr* finally get a blip around midnight. For just three minutes out of a 12-hour dive, sensors detect heat in the water. It isn't much heat, just 32°F (.2°C)—less than most humans would notice—but down in the frigid depths it is massive. The crew hauls the equipment back on board and anxiously develops the photographs *Angus*'s cameras have taken. What they find is beyond their wildest expectations. They have stumbled across a scientific revolution.

Huge concentrations of life weren't supposed to be possible in the deep ocean. No light reaches here, and the pressure is crushing. But photographs don't lie. Nestled comfortably in the volcanic cracks, with boiling water pouring out from the seafloor, was life. Impossible, unimaginable, incomprehensible life.

Over the next days and weeks the scientists aboard the *Knorr* found several vents, and at each one there were new and amazing forms of life.

The scientists saw giant clams the size of dinner plates, huge mussels close to a foot long (30.5 cm), swarms of white brachyuran and galatheid crabs, and most famous of all, huge thickets of red-headed tubeworms as tall as a man.

Science doesn't always follow a clear-cut path. Sometimes discoveries happen that completely derail everything we thought we knew. Think of Galileo and the discovery that Earth orbits the sun, not the other way around, or Charles Darwin, whose theory of

These massive *Calyptogena* clams (above and right) may look pretty, but they smell terrible. The hydrogen sulfide they absorb from vent fluid makes them smell like rotten eggs.

Black smokers (right), the hottest and most powerful kind of vent, spew out massive clouds of metal and minerals.

BLACK SMOKER

AN EXTREMELY HOT
HYDROTHERMAL VENT
NAMED FOR ITS MASSIVE
PLUME OF MINERAL-
RICH BLACK SMOKE

11

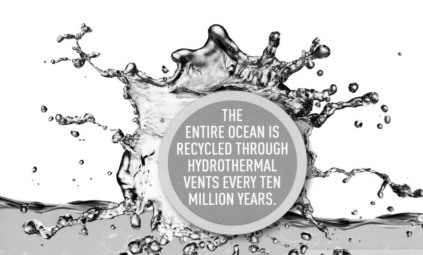

evolution took biology into completely new and unexpected directions. Scientific revolutions happen when we stop seeing the world we expect and start seeing the world as it is.

The incredible biological world of the vents may never have been discovered had scientists not been trying to solve a geological puzzle.

Earth's tectonic plates float like bath toys on top of a massive liquid mantle. In some places they expand and create vents, volcanoes, and new seafloor; in others old seafloor is destroyed. The ocean itself also cycles through the hydrothermal vents at these borders every ten million years, which is what gives the ocean its salty taste. At research sites around the world, scientists are trying to unravel the mystery of the deep vents. Like those on the Galápagos Rift (enlarged map), each one holds more clues. But in an ocean covering almost 140 million square miles (225 million sq km) it will take decades for more scientists to find all the answers.

ARCTIC OCEAN

Eurasian Plate

EUROPE

A S I A

Arabian Plate

AFRICA

African Plate

Indian Plate

Philippine Plate

Pacific Plate

EQUATOR

INDIAN OCEAN

AUSTRALIA

Southwest Indian Ridge

Southeast Indian Ridge

Australian Plate

Antarctic Plate

ANTARCTICA

MAP KEY
— Plate boundary
• Research site

Today, we know that Earth's crust is broken into great slabs called plates that travel across the planet's surface as though on some sort of slow-moving conveyor belt. The complex interaction of these plates is called plate tectonics, and it is the force behind mountain building, volcanic and earthquake activity, and the slow reshaping of Earth's continents and oceans.

Back in the 1970s, though, this idea was still in its infancy, and the biggest question was what powered this "belt." Geologists reasoned that the only heat source powerful enough to move continent-size blocks of Earth's crust was liquid rock, or magma, in the mantle. At places where two plates were pulling apart, known as spreading centers, geologists thought that heat from the mantle would break through as a sort of exhaust system for Earth's core. Finding that heat would be an amazing geological discovery.

In the early 1970s, during a search on the Mid-Atlantic Ridge, scientists found lots of evidence for plate tectonics, but none of the hot water they were expecting. Undeterred, geologists John Corliss and Bob Ballard decided to try again in 1977 on a mission funded in part by the National

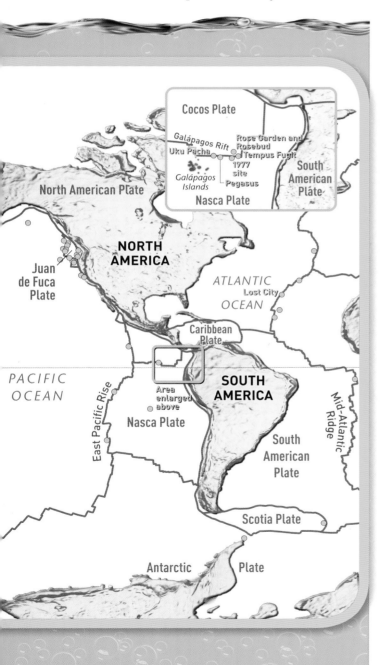

FINDING THAT HEAT WOULD BE AN AMAZING GEOLOGICAL DISCOVERY.

Geographic Society. This time, they were looking in the Pacific in an isolated area known as the Galápagos Rift. Spreading along the Galápagos Rift is much faster than it is along the Mid-Atlantic Ridge. The hope was that the faster-moving areas would release more heat and generate more vents. They had no idea how right they were or what this would mean for studying the deep sea.

Before that day in February, biologists had reason to believe that the deep ocean was an almost lifeless desert populated by a few scavengers that

HYDROTHERMAL VENTS

Hydrothermal vents are geysers and hot springs on the seafloor that form where Earth's crust is spreading apart. These vents are like icebergs. The astounding worlds that they support on the seafloor are just the tip of what lies hidden below—a whole network of cracks and channels connected to the system's fiery heart inside Earth.

Here's how vents work. **1** Cold seawater seeps down through cracks in the ocean floor. **2** As gravity pulls the water deeper into Earth's crust, energy from molten rock deep beneath the seafloor heats the water to 650°F–700°F (343°C–371°C). **3** As the water gets hotter, chemical reactions change the water. It picks up dissolved metals, including iron, copper, and zinc; loses its oxygen; and picks up hydrogen sulfide. The super-hot water rises rapidly back to the surface, carrying with it the dissolved metals and hydrogen sulfide. **4** It mixes with cold seawater as it exits the vent.

In black smokers, the most powerful kind of vent, "smoke" gushes out of a chimney-like opening. The smoke is actually bits of metallic sulfide, which is black. White smokers gush different elements and are cooler and less powerful. Coolest and weakest of all are the diffuse vents. Fluid in these vents mixes with seawater and spreads out before emerging onto the seafloor.

might be able to live on the remains of animals or plants that dropped from the surface. At the time, photosynthesis—the process by which plants combine air and sunlight to create sugar for food—was the base of every food chain known to science. But sunlight fades quickly in the ocean. Dive down just 650 feet (198 m), and 90 percent of the light from the surface disappears. Below about 200 feet (61 m), there's not enough light for photosynthesis to happen. No photosynthesis, scientists thought, meant no great concentrations of life.

With the discovery of the amazing creatures at the vents, scientists had to toss out the assumed limits of life. Here were creatures that could withstand conditions previously thought impossible. The life-forms at the vents weren't just extreme in their environment, they were also extreme in their diet. In a world without light, deep-sea microbes use chemicals from vent water—especially hydrogen sulfide—to create energy. They use this chemical energy

to change carbon dioxide in seawater into sugars that nourish vent life.

The quest to understand the deep ocean is just beginning. All the vents we've discovered so far have been found in less than one percent of the ocean. Exploring this uncharted frontier is the mission of the Office of Oceanic Exploration and Research at the National Oceanic and Atmospheric Administration (NOAA) and its flagship, the *Okeanos Explorer*. In 2011 a team of scientists set out on the *Okeanos* to explore one of the most famous hydrothermal hunting grounds on the planet: the Galápagos Rift.

LIKE SNOWFLAKES, NO TWO DEEP-SEA HYDROTHERMAL VENTS ARE EXACTLY ALIKE.

These clouds of water spewing from inside Earth contain billions of microorganisms that provide food for most vent life.

A cable transmits power and commands from the ship to the ROV.

Yellow flotation packs help control the ROV's descent.

URI

INSTITUTE FOR EXPLORATION
Mystic Aquarium

NATIONAL GEOGRAPHIC

ROVs carry powerful lights, cameras, and acoustic sensors onboard.

TELEPRESENCE

THE ABILITY TO EXPLORE REMOTE AREAS IN REAL TIME BY USING HUMAN-GUIDED VEHICLES AND OTHER TECHNOLOGY

EXPLORING THE ABYSS

SIX HUNDRED MILES (966 KM) OFF the west coast of South America, the *Okeanos Explorer* looks like a small white dot on a vast blue ocean. The only indications of something extraordinary happening here are the number of people in hard hats on the aft deck and the cable dangling into the water.

Eight thousand feet (2.4 km) below the ship is the remotely operated vehicle (ROV) *Little Hercules*, a blocky yellow vehicle with camera eyes. Its partner, a camera-and-lighting platform named *Seirios*, hovers above it. The robotic companions, guided by pilots onboard the *Okeanos*, have been falling for more than an hour and a half and still have not reached the seafloor. Their target: an area on the Galápagos Rift called 2-A, just a few hundred miles from where the first hydrothermal vents were discovered in 1977. One month before, the *Okeanos* had mapped the area using remote sensors and had detected heat and a distinct chemical signature in the water— strong signs of a vent. Expectations are high.

For mission director Tim Shank, a biologist from Woods Hole Oceanographic Institution,

ROVs like *Little Hercules* are the workhorses of modern oceanography. Fiber-optic cable several miles long allows scientists on the surface to see and guide the vehicle's every move as if they were there.

17

MISSING THE SMALLEST CLUE COULD MEAN MISSING A VENT ENTIRELY.

The volcanic landscape is awash in the black debris of past eruptions, lava tubes, and a type of volcanic rock called basalt, but after several hours of searching, no vents are found. The glossy black basalt, though, gives them hope. There was an eruption here not too long ago.

Exploring the deep ocean is an exercise in humility, and no one knows this better than Tim Shank. With more than 20 years in research, 50-plus dives in submarines, and hundreds using ROVs, he's been on missions in every major ocean basin and many smaller

and the ROV team from NOAA, the heart of the operation is the command center deep inside the ship. In the darkened room, faces of the pilots, navigators, and scientists glow in the reflected light of more than two dozen computer and video monitors. Live images from the ROV and camera sled cover an entire wall and are beamed out live to scientists worldwide.

As the distance to the ocean floor tracks toward zero, the first images seem promising. The water is so thick with smoke and silt that it's hard to see anything else. A powerful hydrothermal vent should be in the area. For the vehicles and crew, the search is on.

Unfortunately, finding a vent isn't as easy as following its smoke. Down in the depths, a layer of pressure known as a barocline forms an invisible barrier. When vent smoke hits this layer, it scatters over a wide area, obscuring the source. To find the vent, Tim and his team will have to read the signs in the landscape.

Everything from the shape and color of the rocks, to the amount of "stuff" floating in the water, to the number of crabs wandering around can influence the direction of a search. Missing the smallest clue could mean missing a vent entirely.

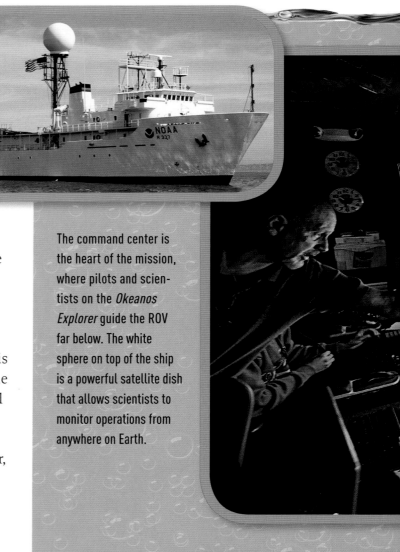

The command center is the heart of the mission, where pilots and scientists on the *Okeanos Explorer* guide the ROV far below. The white sphere on top of the ship is a powerful satellite dish that allows scientists to monitor operations from anywhere on Earth.

seas and has seen almost every type of vent that we know of. Despite all his experience and that of the *Okeanos* crew, the hunt for new hydrothermal vents is never easy. Identifying targets is an art as much as a science. It's a big ocean, and hydrothermal vents can be as small as your living room. Sometimes, as with the just completed dive on 2-A, even the best guesses go wrong.

For two days *Little Herc* and *Seirios* explore the rest of 2-A in search of the vent that created so much smoke, but with no luck. Finally, on the third day, winding along troughs

WE KNOW MORE ABOUT THE SURFACE OF MARS THAN WE DO ABOUT THE DEEP OCEAN.

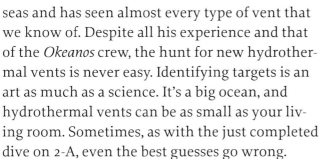

at the bottom of a rocky cliff face, signs of vents begin to appear on screens in the ship's command center.

Most rocks in the ocean are covered with the remains of plants and animals that float down from the surface. Biologists call this "marine snow." But the rocks on the screens, with their large patches of orange and white, are far different. The orange color is iron oxide, commonly known as rust. It forms when hot vent water interacts with iron in the rocks. The white patches are mats made up of huge numbers of tiny microbes spewed out of the vent. The water flowing out of cracks in the ocean floor shimmers in the ROV's lights. Straight ahead is the mission's first hydrothermal vent.

It isn't a black smoker with massive chimneys and elegant spires, or a fully mature vent teeming with life. It's even more rare. It's a young vent with water flowing from just a few stained cracks in the ocean floor. Unlike the superheated water blasted out of black smokers, the water here is about 60°F (15.6°C). It may not look like much, but only a handful of vents this young have ever been found.

The life here is simple and small, mostly microbes, microscopic organisms from inside Earth. These microbes will form the base of the food chain and support tubeworms, shrimp, crabs, and other creatures that will colonize the vent. The absence of such creatures is a sign that this vent may be only a few weeks or months old. Scientists still don't know exactly how life forms or arrives at vents or when colonization begins. Watching this vent grow up could add volumes to what they know about how vent life develops.

SPIRES OF SOME BLACK SMOKER VENTS CAN GROW AS MUCH AS A FOOT A DAY.

SUDDENLY IMAGES OF TOWERING VENT SPIRES RISING FROM THE SEAFLOOR APPEAR ON THE MONITORS LIKE GHOSTLY REVELATIONS.

The shape of each vent is unique and depends on the chemistry of the vent, the force of the eruption, and more. Some are shaped like pipe organs, others like chimneys. The top of this one looks like a beehive.

CHIMNEYS

GIANT TOWERS OF METALS AND MINERALS CREATED BY THE RESIDUE OF BLACK SMOKER VENTS

The team names the vent Uku Pacha, after the Inca underworld god of death and rebirth, then orders *Little Herc* to move on. The decision seems to pay off. Sonar sensors on *Seirios* detect massive structures ahead. Suddenly images of towering vent spires rising from the seafloor appear on the monitors like ghostly revelations. The lumpy, mottled spires of iron, rock, and sulfur are the exhaust vents of the volcanic world deep within Earth.

One of them is the tallest spire ever found in the Galápagos Rift, rising more than 100 feet (30.5 m) into the sea. Other chimneys connected to the same powerful vent below loom in the darkness beyond. White crabs about six inches (15.2 cm) long crawl up the formations, providing the awed onlookers with a sense of scale. The massive, multistory towers look like the industrial smokestacks of some alien world.

Huge chimneys are only associated with powerful and long-lasting smoker vents. Building a spire like this would have taken decades, even a century or more. Unfortunately, this hydrothermal vent is dead and has been for decades. Thirty years ago this black smoker would have been a billowing inferno with a thriving ecosystem around it. But not anymore.

GETTING INTO THE DEEP

1

2

3

4

There are four ways to explore the deep sea:

SUBMERSIBLES

Battery-powered submersibles are the only way for people to physically visit the deep sea. Pilots and scientists kneel or lie down inside a steel sphere looking out fist-size windows to explore or to collect samples. To make sure the multi-ton submersible doesn't sink, air-filled spheres neutralize the weight, allowing the craft to float easily in the water. Robotic arms enable the pilot to interact with the outside world.

CAMERA SLEDS

These sleek craft are the underwater equivalent of eyes in the sky. High-definition cameras and powerful LED lights can light up the deep and take pictures of the wonders below, while side-scan sonar creates amazingly detailed maps. The images and electricity are transmitted through a cable attached to the ship. When paired with an ROV, a sled also acts as a shock absorber, isolating the ROV from the movement of waves at the surface.

AUTONOMOUS UNDERWATER VEHICLES (AUVS)

Like a camera sled, but without a cable, these machines are programmed from the surface to head out and explore the deep on their own. They follow a pre-planned route, using onboard sensors and sonar to record data before returning to the mother ship to share their findings with scientists.

REMOTELY OPERATED VEHICLES (ROVS)

Piloted from mother ships on the surface via long cables, these vehicles are able to explore the depths by remote control. They are the workhorses of the oceanographic fleet. Using onboard lights and real-time cameras for eyes and robotic manipulators for hands, they are able to collect samples of the biology and geology of the deep. Thrusters allow them to move in virtually any direction with ease.

The vehicles continue to scour the area, hoping to find the source of the smoke they saw on the first dive, but with no luck. After a few hours, they return to the surface and move on.

The next day the team has a new target—2-C—and from the images being relayed by *Seirios* and *Little Herc* it looks like they have found the vent they were looking for. The bottom below the vehicles has the deep and bulbous blackness of new and fresh lava. Even better, it has the white staining only deposited by boiling water seeping through cracks in the ocean floor. What looks like snow is actually a blizzard of microbes being shot out of a vent like snow out of a snowblower.

Like the Uku Pacha vent, this one, which they name Pegasus, is a young diffuse vent but with more life. The clouds of microbes have attracted shrimp, crabs, and snails to the vent. As long as they have food to eat, they will stay and multiply. Missing are the tubeworms. They are called sessile animals because they spend their whole lives physically attached to a vent. It's a sign that this vent, although perhaps older than the one at 2-A, is still extremely young.

For Tim and his team, finding one new young vent is a great accomplishment. Finding two this close together may indicate something more is going on.

VENT MICROBES CAN BE USED TO CLEAN UP OIL SPILLS AND TOXIC WASTE ON EARTH'S SURFACE.

Hydrothermal vent fluid is packed with bits of minerals and microbes. Clouds of these organisms can create a snow-blower effect that makes seeing the actual vent difficult.

MICROBE

A MICROSCOPIC ORGANISM THAT USUALLY HAS JUST ONE CELL

Scientists often use crabs as clues to find vents.

Brachyuran crabs will fight and even eat each other over access to vents.

SESSILE

PLANTS OR ANIMALS THAT ARE PERMANENTLY FIXED TO A PLACE

24

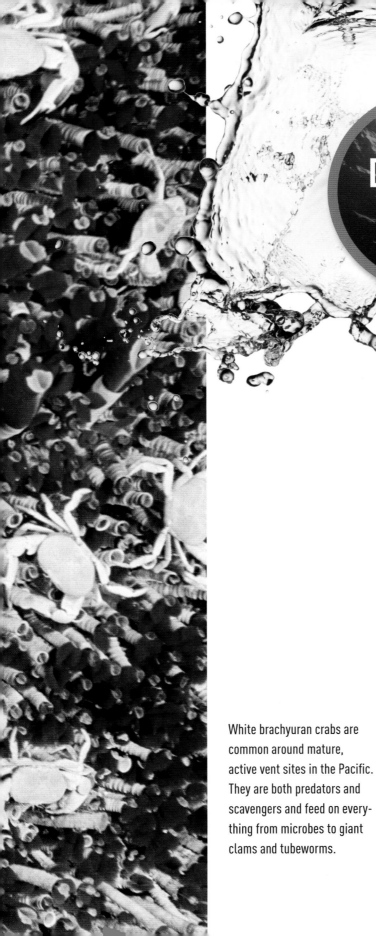

White brachyuran crabs are common around mature, active vent sites in the Pacific. They are both predators and scavengers and feed on everything from microbes to giant clams and tubeworms.

LIFE & DEATH ON THE VENTS

TWO WEEKS INTO THE CRUISE, TIM AND the scientists aboard the *Okeanos Explorer* have already made some great discoveries: one of the youngest vents, one of the tallest chimney spires ever found on the Galápagos Rift, and massive fields of fresh lava on almost every dive.

Hydrothermal vents go through periods of boom and bust: sometimes flourishing with amazing life and sometimes looking like wastelands. The cycle of boom and bust is dictated far beneath the surface.

The Galápagos Rift is a spreading center—a place on the ocean floor where two tectonic plates tear apart (see pages 12-13), allowing fresh magma from Earth's mantle to rush in and fill the gap. The wider the tear, the more molten rock escapes from the mantle. The more that happens, the more volcanic and hydrothermal activity there is. The Galápagos Rift was thought to be steady and stable. In dozens of cruises over a 20-year period, scientists never saw a single eruption or baby vent. The *Okeanos* team has already found two baby vents—one weeks old, one months old—and miles of new lava.

But while the discoveries are amazing, understanding how vents grow requires visiting known vents several times to watch them develop and change. Because scientists can't stay in the deep ocean permanently, they can only take "snapshots" of time to reveal those changes. Collect enough of those snapshots, and scientists can piece together the life of a vent. A well-known vent field called Rosebud is nearby and offers the team a chance to get more data on vents over time.

EXPLORING THE OCEAN IS LIKE WANDERING IN THE DARK WITH A FLASHLIGHT.

There's another reason to dive on Rosebud. The Galápagos Rift is changing; Rosebud could be changing with it.

Tim is no stranger to the Rosebud vents. He was the chief scientist on the expedition that discovered them in 2002, and he has seen them both physically in the *Alvin* submersible and virtually at the helm of ROV dives. Rosebud was thought to be just three years old the first time he saw it.

As *Little Herc* approaches the site, Tim and the

Death in the ocean isn't the end. Food is scarce, so nothing in the ocean is wasted. These dead tube-worms (above) will create a feast for scavenging crabs and jelly-like siphonophores.

others anxiously watch the monitors for views of an active vent teeming with life. What greets them is shocking. Rosebud is missing.

There are no empty tubeworm tubes, no clamshells, no ghostly spires—nothing. One of the most famous hydrothermal vent sites appears to have disappeared. The scientists scramble for an explanation. Perhaps the navigation is off. Exploring the ocean is like wandering in the dark with a flashlight. It's easy to miss something, even something the size of a hydrothermal vent.

But when the team directs *Little Herc* and *Seirios* to the top of a nearby mountain to get their bearings, everything seems to check out.

90 PERCENT OF ALL VOLCANIC ACTIVITY ON EARTH TAKES PLACE IN THE OCEAN.

Pillow basalt (left) forms when lava squeezes out from openings in the seafloor as though flowing from a tube of toothpaste. Fresh basalt can be a great clue for finding recent eruptions and hydrothermal vents.

BASALT

A TYPE OF VOLCANIC ROCK THAT MAKES UP MOST OF THE OCEAN FLOOR

GROWING OUT OF THE VENTS WAS A MASSIVE HEDGE OF WHITE "STREAKS" UP TO 12 FEET TALL.

SOME TUBEWORMS CAN GROW ALMOST FIVE FEET (1.5 M) IN LESS THAN TWO YEARS.

Tubeworms grow up fast. The young ones above are only a few inches long. In less than two years they can reach five feet (1.5 m) or more. The one being held by Tim Shank (far right) and some coworkers at Woods Hole Oceanographic Institution is almost eight feet (2.4 m) long.

Over the next several hours, they set up a systematic search of the area, but the only thing they find is massive sheets of fresh lava. Either the scientists are truly lost in the dark ocean or Rosebud has disappeared since it was last visited in 2005.

A creeping sense of déjà vu comes over the crew. You see, Rosebud isn't the first vent on the Galápagos Rift to disappear.

The Rose Garden vents were among the first ever discovered. They were a crown jewel of the oceanographic world. At first sight the vents looked like the creation of some crazed painter.

Growing out of them was a massive hedge of white "streaks" up to 12 feet tall (3.7 m) and several inches thick. The streaks—each topped by a red plume—were the now familiar tubeworms (*Riftia pachyptila*). Each one was positioned to reach the fluid erupting from the vent. Scientists returned year after year to study these animals.

Nothing amazed them more than to find out that tubeworms have no gut and no butt. In fact they didn't seem to have any digestive system at all. How do they eat? Scientists were clueless until they discovered that tubeworms "team up" with

HYDROTHERMAL VENTS AND THE ANIMALS THAT THEY SUPPORT LIVE ON BORROWED TIME IN A WORLD OF TICKING TIME BOMBS.

vent bacteria in what's known as a symbiotic relationship. This means that both the bacteria and the worm depend on each other for survival. A special sac inside the tubeworm provides a safe environment for the bacteria. In exchange, the bacteria convert chemicals in the vent fluid into sugars that nourish the tubeworm. Life varies from vent to vent, but all of it relies on these bacteria to turn chemicals into food.

Rose Garden was an awe-inspiring place, but it wasn't to last.

On a 2002 visit Tim was in *Alvin*. Then as today, the crew went down, and then as today, the vents were nowhere to be found. Instead all around was fresh black lava.

The beating volcanic heart that powered the hydrothermal wonderland had erupted, burying the famous vents and all the tubeworms and other life-forms beneath massive piles of lava. Nearby, the crew found a new vent with younger versions of the life they had seen at Rose Garden. The scientists named it Rosebud in honor of its famous forefather. Now Rosebud too is missing.

From observing phenomenon like this, scientists have learned that hydrothermal vent systems have definite and distinct life spans as complete and diverse as yours and mine. They are born, they grow, and they die. When vents die, though, they don't go alone. All the animals that rely on

Shallow-water crabs, like this one (right), find protection from predators by living with anemones. Like tubeworms, mussels (below) need bacteria but have other ways of getting food. This means that they can survive both in and away from a vent.

SYMBIOSIS

TWO DIFFERENT SPECIES LIVING TOGETHER FOR THE BENEFIT OF ONE OR BOTH OF THE ORGANISMS

them—from the tiny microbes to the mussels, tubeworms, and massive clams—die with them.

Hydrothermal vents and the animals that they support live on borrowed time in a world of ticking time bombs. Just the slightest change in the underground plumbing that powers a vent can lead to its extinction or death. The only way for the organisms that live on and around the vents to survive and thrive is to grow up fast and have a lot of offspring.

After hours of searching the Rosebud site, the team found only one hopeful sign that life might still be in the area: mussels, living at the border of the fresh lava but far from an active vent. Had these been pushed by the lava from Rosebud to a new home? Scientists had seen other mussels that rode lava flows hundreds of yards away from a vent. Were these all that remained of Rosebud? If so, they were a grave reminder of the temporary nature of most vents and the power of the magma chambers beneath.

As the day wound down, *Seirios* and *Little Herc* returned to the surface and were hoisted onto the back deck of the ship. The visit to Rosebud, although far from what Tim and the others had expected, had given them new insight into what they had found at Uku Pacha and Pegasus. The team was anxious to see what the next day's dive would reveal.

THERE ARE ABOUT 285 BILLION BACTERIA IN EVERY OUNCE OF TISSUE IN A TUBEWORM.

Anemones use their tentacles for defense or to sting prey for eating.

Most sea anemones are sessile, meaning they will spend their whole lives in the same place.

SPECIES

A UNIT OF CLASSIFICATION FOR ORGANISMS WITH SIMILAR CHARACTERISTICS THAT CAN BREED WITH ONE ANOTHER

A VENT WORTH WAITING FOR

Beautiful sea anemones like this one were just one of the amazing animals Tim and the team on the *Okeanos* saw when they discovered the Tempus Fugit hydrothermal vent on the ninth dive of the expedition.

VOLCANIC ACTIVITY HAS LITERALLY reshaped the Galápagos Rift. Well-studied vents that had existed for years have disappeared, and new vents have been found where none had existed. The realization that a new boom time for vents has begun on the rift heightens the sense of excitement in the control room as the team prepares to dive on a new target: site 4-A West, on the far eastern end of the rift. Would they find an amazing flowering of new life, a place where life had been destroyed, or something completely different? As *Little Herc* and *Seirios* reach the seafloor, 8,400 feet (2,560 m) below the surface, the search begins again.

The vehicles transmit images as they glide along fissures and faults in the ocean floor. The location looks perfect for vents, and the water starts filling up with the snowflake-like particles seen at other sites. The scientists even see increasing numbers of brachyuran crabs, a good sign that vents are nearby. Suddenly they reach the edge of a cliff, and the only thing visible is a polychaete worm swimming in the distance. This worm, which breathes through long tendrils that

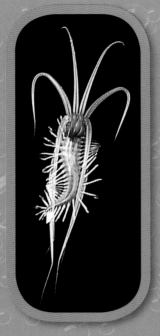

The Tempus Fugit vent had an amazing array of animal diversity, from swimming polychaete worms (above) to tubeworms (top, right) and anemones (bottom, right).

DIFFUSE VENT

A HYDROTHERMAL VENT WITH COOLER FLUID THAT EXITS FROM SEVERAL OPENINGS ON THE SEAFLOOR

hydrothermal vents: white clamshells the size of dinner plates (see page 10). But first impressions can be deceiving, so the vehicles move in for a closer look. They're vent clams all right, but the shells are empty and riddled with holes. Judging by the condition of the shells, Tim guesses that the clams died with the vent 20 years ago.

The disappointment is short-lived. There's smoke in the water just ahead. Then one by one other key signs of the presence of a vent appear: debris in the water, crabs, and staining on the rocks. Finally Tim sees what they all have been waiting for: tubeworms.

Standing like sentinels are two small tube-worms just over two feet tall (.6 m), their frilly red plumes waving in the upwelling current. Shimmering water flows around them from stained cracks in the seafloor. Anemones cover the rocks like chicken pox. Snails crawl slowly over the surface, cleaning the rocks and munching on the microbial "snow" erupting from the vent. Live mussels the size of Tim's thumb are wedged into the rocks. It's a diffuse vent similar to Uku Pacha and Pegasus but on a completely different scale. The small size of the vent animals means that this is another young field—maybe younger than Rosebud when it was discovered.

For the team on the *Okeanos* it is a fantastic moment. They are nine dives into a search for new features and vents on the most famous hydrothermal hunting ground on the planet,

drift in the water, is a reminder that even without the hydrothermal vents, life can exist at this depth.

Little Herc and *Seirios* push on, diving down the sheer edge of a rock face about five stories tall, to reconnect with the ocean floor. There, nestled in the volcanic rock at the base of the cliff, they find something that exists only at

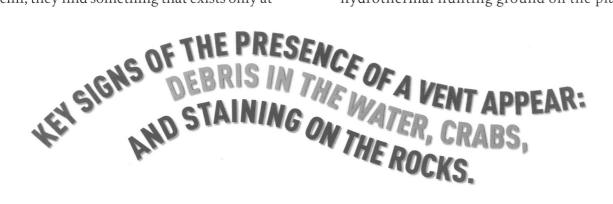

KEY SIGNS OF THE PRESENCE OF A VENT APPEAR: DEBRIS IN THE WATER, CRABS, AND STAINING ON THE ROCKS.

and they have finally found a fully functioning vent ecosystem.

In some places, the water is flowing out in the "snowblower" effect they'd seen at the Pegasus vents. In others, piles of raw sulfur that has been ejected by the vent are scattered about, looking like discarded barbecue potato chips. Mysterious white "fluffy stuff" is sprawled across the rocks like a network of cotton candy fibers.

The discovery is intoxicating. The vent isn't just new, it is also big—one of the largest ever discovered on the Galápagos Rift. It covers more than an acre of ground, with life on almost every part of it. For the next two days everyone in the command center spends hours glued to the screens. They watch crabs battle over access to the vents and shrimp dart in and out of cracks in the ocean floor. In all, they count more than 13 species of animals wandering the vent field, from mussels and tubeworms sitting directly in the vent water to clusters of scavenging dandelion siphonophores and anemones that ring the outer edge. They even find one type of tubeworm—the *Tevnia*—that had only been found in a completely different section of the ocean more than a thousand miles away (see Biogeography, page 38).

Everything points to the youth of this vent, with one notable exception: the empty clamshells riddled with holes. Tim and the team estimate that it would have taken decades after the vent died for the clams to reach this state of decay. For the crew it's an amazing paradox: The site is both decades old and long dead but also brand-new and full of life. So what happened?

The only answer that makes sense is that the vent has rebooted. Somehow, the underground plumbing network of cracks and fissures that brings vent fluid to the surface must have

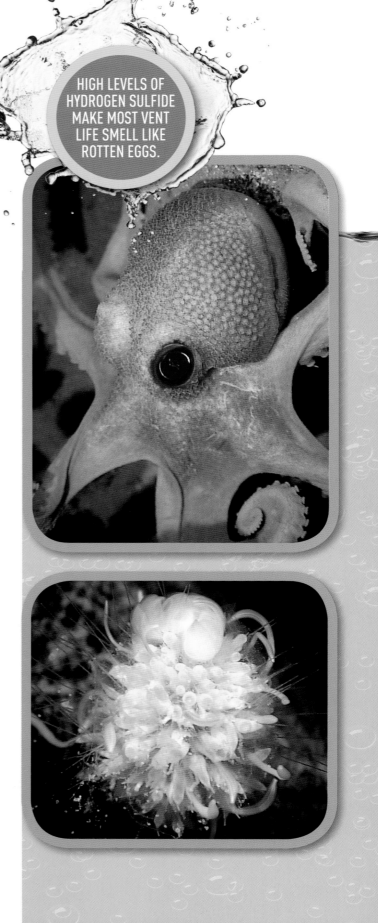

HIGH LEVELS OF HYDROGEN SULFIDE MAKE MOST VENT LIFE SMELL LIKE ROTTEN EGGS.

ECOSYSTEM

A GROUP OF DIVERSE ORGANISMS THAT INTERACT IN A SINGLE ENVIRONMENT

Healthy vents don't have just small creatures; they also have top predators like the octopus (opposite, top). Scavengers like the dandelion siphonophore (opposite, bottom) ringed the outer edge of the Tempus Fugit vent along with the occasional sea spider (above, left). Even the beautifully colored holothurian, or sea cucumber (above, right), can be found among the extraordinary quantity of life around an active vent. Deep-sea hydrothermal vents can have up to 10,000 times more life than the regular seafloor.

BIOGEOGRAPHY

The study of why different animals live in different places is called biogeography, and it's one of the key areas in ocean science. You see, the ocean isn't just one massive body of water. Like continents, it can be divided into several different ecosystems. Just as you only find giraffes in Africa and llamas in South America, life in the deep is divided the same way. Scientists currently divide the deep ocean into six distinct regions, all of which have their own types of animals.

Scientists still don't understand what causes the divisions, especially when the ocean water, the basalt of the ocean floor, and even the vent fluid is pretty much the same everywhere. But in the Pacific Ocean tubeworms and brachyuran crabs predominate, while the Atlantic vents can have tens of thousands of shrimp. In the Southern Ocean around Antarctica strange hairy crustaceans known as yeti crabs can be found, while the Indian Ocean has a strange mixture of the Atlantic and Pacific creatures.

Unlike the continents on the surface, which have clear barriers, borders in the abyss are much less clear. Understanding why these areas form and what their borders are is a key link in learning how the deep ocean works and how the strange world of the hydrothermal vents began.

Massive swarms of shrimp are common in the Atlantic Ocean.

Galatheid crabs live on seamounts in the western Pacific Ocean.

Strange hairy crabs dominate the Southern Ocean.

The medusa jellyfish can be found in the Arctic Ocean.

survived even when the volcanic power source cooled. Now that magma from the mantle has moved back in and restarted everything, boom times are back on the rift. But the empty clamshells are a solemn reminder of the fate that ultimately awaits all life at deep-sea hydrothermal vents. These vents might be able to reboot, but the life around them dies or moves on in the meantime. It's impossible to know whether a vent will last for decades, centuries, or millennia or whether it can ever be resurrected. Fully aware that time is precious—and fleeting—for life on a hydrothermal vent, the team names the field Tempus Fugit, which is Latin for "time is fleeting."

Tempus Fugit is hands down the great discovery of the voyage, but there are some lingering questions. The scientists still don't know just when the various new vents they have seen were created, or why the changes on the rift happened across such a wide area—Uku Pacha and Tempus Fugit are almost 150 miles (241 km) apart.

Tim and the team believe that the changes are being caused by something called a dike injection. This happens when magma moves into new cracks, fissures, and tubes without erupting. It often occurs when tectonic plates tear apart and new cracks form in Earth's crust. If any of these cracks pierce a magma chamber in the mantle, the chamber will erupt like a popped water balloon, causing molten rock to spread out through the crack.

Finding out exactly how many vents this new surge of activity has created, reactivated, or destroyed will be the work of future expeditions. For Tim and his team there is a sense of mission accomplished. They had set out to find new vents and new forms of life, and they have done just that.

Some of the stromatolite fossils found at Shark Bay are more than three billion years old.

Some stromatolites still occur today in super salty lakes and pools.

ARCHAEA

A UNIQUE TYPE OF MICROORGANISM THAT IS THE OLDEST KNOWN FORM OF LIFE ON EARTH

THE ORIGIN OF LIFE?

SO WHAT DOES THIS ALIEN DEEP-SEA world have to do with you and me and the rest of life at the surface? The answer just might be, "Everything." You, your dog, the plants, the animals, and even the paper in this book all may have gotten their start billions of years ago in the strange world of deep-sea vents. It may seem crazy, but it's not as far-fetched as it sounds.

Scientists have long believed that life began in the ocean. The stromatolites found in the shallows of Shark Bay, Australia, might look like rocks, but they are actually fossilized remains of some of the oldest life-forms on Earth. Inside them, streaks of white reveal places where ancient microbes gathered. Known as Archaea, these microorganisms made up most of the life we know about for the first 3.5 billion years of Earth's existence.

For almost all of Earth's 4.5-billion-year history, the only life was ocean life. But finding out where or even what type of place in the ocean life began is much more complicated.

While no one has managed to create life, scientists do know that its building blocks are

This may look like a rocky cove, but these rocks are actually stromatolites, massive communities of microorganisms trapped between layers of sand and rock.

pretty simple: some basic chemistry, including methane, oxygen, and carbon; an ecosystem stable enough for life to thrive and spread; and—most important—water.

In the early days of Earth, the planet's surface was anything but stable. Asteroids and comets constantly pummeled the surface. Life could not have survived long enough there to develop the process of photosynthesis to sustain it. But deep-sea hydrothermal vents would have had all the necessary ingredients for life—life that relied on chemosynthesis rather than photosynthesis.

Hydrothermal vents existed as soon as liquid water accumulated on Earth more than 4.2 billion years ago. As the ocean grew deeper, it would have insulated the vents from the bombardment going on at the surface, and its currents would have helped spread the new life from vent to vent.

But as the Rose Garden, Rosebud, and Tempus Fugit vents show, the life of a hydrothermal vent is usually pretty brief, with most lasting only decades. Scientists needed to find a vent that had been stable for tens of thousands of years—long enough to allow life to begin, grow, and spread out.

In 2000 Deborah Kelley, a professor at the University of Washington and a colleague of Tim, found just that. She was chief scientist on the expedition that discovered a vent now known as Lost City. It was the strangest vent field anyone

SCIENTISTS NEEDED TO FIND A VENT THAT HAD BEEN STABLE FOR TENS OF THOUSANDS OF YEARS—LONG ENOUGH FOR LIFE TO BEGIN, GROW, AND SPREAD OUT.

These soaring spires of the Lost City hydrothermal vent field, illuminated here by ROV lights, reveal the astonishing scale of the system's carbonite towers. The intense darkness of the deep means that seeing the full field is possible only through sonar mapping.

SONAR MAPPING

THE USE OF SOUND WAVES TO CREATE A THREE-DIMENSIONAL MAP OF A DEEP-SEA LOCATION

had yet seen in any part of the world's ocean.

In place of bulging black smoker chimneys were dozens of delicate, cathedral-like spires of calcium carbonate, a compound commonly found in baking soda. Each was packed with new forms of life. More than half of the species the scientists saw had never been seen before.

The water coming out of the vents was only 175°F (79°C)—about 500 degrees (277°C) cooler than at some black smokers. Strangest of all, the system wasn't powered by seawater interacting with magma deep inside Earth. The team learned that the heat creating and supporting the Lost City vents comes from a chemical reaction of seawater and a rock in the mantle called olivine. When olivine reacts with seawater in a process called serpentinization, it creates a great deal of heat, methane, and other minerals that come streaming up to the surface of the seafloor. From Lost City's size, scientists estimate that this process has been at work here for more than 30,000 years.

Kelley and her team discovered a completely new deep-sea ecosystem. Another surprise: A thin film of Archaea lined the vent. The life at Lost City isn't swimming around in the acidic flow of a volcanic stream as on the Galápagos Rift. Instead the water here is highly alkaline—the opposite of acidic—and chemically closer to bleach. Scientists never thought life was possible

43

ALIENS AMONG US

The deep sea and deep space may not seem like natural companions, but the secrets found in the innermost depths of the ocean may provide clues to unlocking one of the greatest mysteries in the universe: Are we alone?

Some of the smallest creatures found at hydrothermal vents may help solve the riddle. Hidden inside these vents are microorganisms known as extremophiles: organisms that thrive in environments that would be deadly to most life as we know it. Whether the environment is on the verge of boiling or under crushing pressure or extremely acidic or alkaline, life seems to adapt.

Through all the trials and transformations of Earth, these microorganisms have been able to hang on even during periods of mass extinction, when large amounts of life on Earth died off. The vents are the secret to their success. Using three simple ingredients—water, carbon, and an underground heat source—hydrothermal vents can power an entire ecosystem far removed from the sun-powered world at the surface.

For scientists the idea that simple elements can sustain such complex ecosystems offers an intriguing possibility. Earth isn't the only planet in our solar system with that magical combination of heat, water, and carbon. The great geysers of Saturn's moon Enceladus have all these ingredients; so does Jupiter's moon Europa. Mars once did too. In fact, those three ingredients may be common throughout the universe.

While we have been searching the skies for interstellar probes or flying Martians, the most likely aliens may not look like bug-eyed beasts. Instead they may resemble the tiny microscopic creatures hidden in the alien deep.

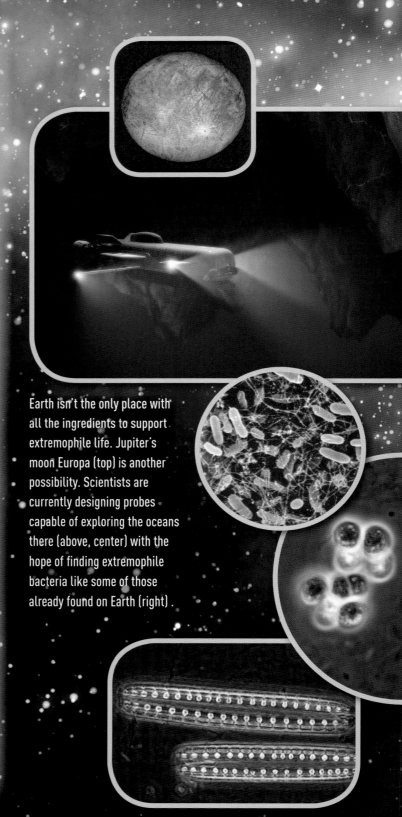

Earth isn't the only place with all the ingredients to support extremophile life. Jupiter's moon Europa (top) is another possibility. Scientists are currently designing probes capable of exploring the oceans there (above, center) with the hope of finding extremophile bacteria like some of those already found on Earth (right).

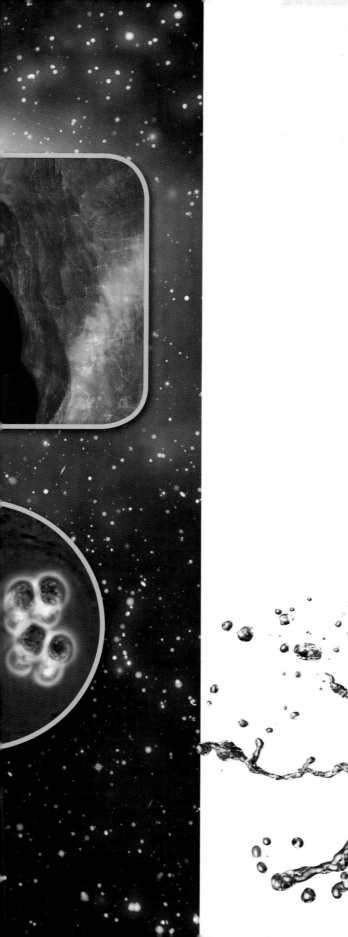

in such an environment until they found it here.

If life could live in environments like Lost City and black smokers, then was there any place too extreme for some form of life not only to survive but also to thrive?

The Archaea and the age of Lost City are tantalizing clues that offer glimpses back to the origin of all life on Earth. But this is not enough. The evidence that life began at hydrothermal vents is mounting, but we haven't proved it yet.

Kelley believes that vents like Lost City can coexist with vents like Tempus Fugit or even black smokers. Such a hybrid world could provide the next step in the search. We just need to find it.

We still don't know the exact environment where life on Earth began. But it is important to recognize that our explorations have already proved that life is possible in environments dominated by crushing pressure, extreme heat, acid baths, and alkaline springs. If life can exist in these extreme environments and if all life—human and otherwise—is made up of the same basic building blocks, is it unreasonable to believe it also exists in worlds beyond our own?

There's only one way to find out: Explore!

GLOSSARY

Abyss
The area of the ocean from 13,000 feet (3,962 m) deep to the ocean floor. This area is often sparsely inhabited except at hydrothermal vents.

Archaea
Microorganisms that belong to an ancient division of life. They are as different from other microorganisms, like bacteria, as they are from humans.

Barocline
An invisible horizontal barrier in the ocean created by pressure.

Basalt
A type of rock created by volcanic eruptions. This rock makes up most of the seafloor.

Black smoker
A chimney-like structure on the seafloor made from metal sulfides, out of which flows hot (~660°F or 349°C) fluids that look like black smoke. The black color of the fluid is due to mineral particles.

Calcium carbonate
The mineral that creates the exoskeletons of corals and the spires of Lost City. It's also the main ingredient in baking soda.

Chemosynthesis
The process by which bacteria use energy from chemicals, such as hydrogen sulfide, combined with water and carbon dioxide to produce sugars.

Extremophile
An organism capable of living in environments that are lethal to most forms of life.

Food chain
The web of connections among animals based on who eats who.

Hydrogen sulfide
A colorless, poisonous gas that smells like rotten eggs.

Hydrothermal vent
A place in the Earth's surface where water heated deep inside Earth erupts onto the surface.

Lava
Melted, or molten, rock is called magma if it is below Earth's surface and lava if it reaches Earth's surface.

Mantle
The 1,800-mile-thick zone (2,897 km) of Earth below the crust and above the core that is made up of minerals, including iron, silica, magnesium, and oxygen.

Marine snow
The steady fall of organic material from the ocean surface to the seafloor. It often includes the bodies or fragments of dead organisms and other waste.

Microbe
An organism, usually consisting of only a single cell, that is visible only with a microscope. Bacteria and Archaea are kinds of microbes.

Mid-Ocean Ridge
The longest mountain chain on the planet, formed at the boundaries of tectonic plates. Molten rock from the mantle below rises to the surface to form hydrothermal vents and new oceanic crust along the ridge.

Photosynthesis
The process by which green plants use energy from the sun to combine water and carbon dioxide to produce carbohydrates and oxygen.

Plate tectonics
The theory that Earth's surface can be divided into a number of plates that move and interact with each other along their boundaries.

Serpentinization
The process that occurs when ocean water interacts with mantle rock. It releases heat, methane, and calcium carbonate.

Sessile
An organism incapable of movement for most of its life. Trees and tubeworms are examples of sessile life-forms.

Siphonophores
A group of marine animals that includes jellyfish and corals. Most are long, thin, and transparent and have many stinging tentacles.

Sonar
Acronym for sound navigation and ranging. Sonar is the method scientists use to determine the distance of objects in the water. It is used to map the ocean floor and to explore using ROVs.

Spreading center
Area where two tectonic plates are moving apart (diverging), opening the seafloor and allowing magma to rise and form new oceanic crust.

Submersible
A human-occupied vehicle that can operate and explore underwater completely independently of a mother ship on the ocean's surface.

Symbiosis (Symbiote)
The close relationship between two different organisms (symbiotes) for the majority of their lives. There are three main kinds: Mutualism benefits both organisms; parasitism benefits one organism at the expense of the other; and commensalism benefits one organism, but the other is neither helped nor harmed.

Telepresence
The idea of using technology to allow people to participate in events without being physically present, such as when scientists onboard a ship use an ROV to explore the ocean or when scientists on shore monitor an expedition.

46

RESOURCES

WEBSITES

National Geographic's Ocean Portal
http://ocean.nationalgeographic.com/ocean
From conservation and exploration to adventure and science, if it's happening in the ocean world, odds are something about it will be found at National Geographic's Ocean portal. Here you will find your favorite underwater animals, whether they are whales, vent shrimp, or the human explorers who seek them.

Ocean Explorer—NOAA
http://oceanexplorer.noaa.gov
The official website of the National Oceanic and Atmospheric Association allows kids to follow the *Okeanos Explorer* in real time, flash through past expeditions (including ones in this book), and build creative and detailed lesson plans corresponding with individual cruises. It also has great breakdowns of the technology in use.

Dive and Discover—Woods Hole Oceanographic Institution
http://www.divediscover.whoi.edu
This ocean portal from Woods Hole Oceanographic Institution allows you to follow scientists in the field, watch expeditions underway, and learn about expeditions on the cutting edge of exploration. It includes videos, an expansive glossary, and teacher resources on every expedition.

Nautilus Live
http://www.nautiluslive.org
Join world-renowned ocean explorer Robert Ballard and his crew aboard the research ship *Nautilus* as they explore the ocean, looking at exotic biology, strange volcanoes, and ancient shipwrecks.

BOOKS

Oceans: Dolphins, Sharks, Penguins, and More!
By Johnna Rizzo
National Geographic Children's Books
March 2010
This fact-filled guide looks at the creatures of the upper ocean, far from the hydrothermal vents below. It is filled with images and explanations of animal characteristics.

Journey into the Deep: Discovering New Ocean Creatures
By Rebecca L. Johnson
Millbrook Press
September 2010
This Orbis Pictus award winner is a great guide to exploring the ocean based on work from the Census of Marine Life, the most extensive investigation into the oceans ever attempted. From the sunlit surface to the strange dark depths, this book will take children on a journey to meet many of the world's exotic creatures.

Weird Sea Creatures
By Laura Marsh
National Geographic Children's Books
August 2012
This brilliantly illustrated book explores the strangest creatures under the sea, including the deep-sea angler fish that has a glowing fishing rod attached to its body.

Ocean: An Illustrated Atlas
By Sylvia A. Earle and Linda K. Glover
National Geographic Books
October 2008
It's hard to wrap your mind around how big the ocean is, but this book will help. Filled with amazing maps and images, it also includes articles written for adults.

The Deep: The Extraordinary Creatures of the Abyss
By Claire Nouvian
University of Chicago Press
March 2007
This vivid photo book looks at the strange and beautiful creatures of the deep ocean. While this book is aimed at adults, children will be mesmerized by the astonishing imagery.

Citizens of the Sea: Wondrous Creatures From the Census of Marine Life
By Nancy Knowlton
National Geographic Books
September 2010
Based on the decade-long research project The Census of Marine Life, this amazing work reveals some of the incredible residents of the world's oceans backed by award-winning photography from National Geographic.

INDEX